Twenty to Make
Knitted
Wrist Warmers

Monica Russel

Search Press

First published in 2014

Search Press Limited
Wellwood, North Farm Road,
Tunbridge Wells, Kent TN2 3DR

Reprinted 2015 (twice)

Text copyright © Monica Russel 2014

Photographs by Fiona Murray Photographic
on location

Photographs and design copyright
© Search Press Ltd 2014

Print ISBN: 978-1-84448-975-6
EPUB ISBN: 978-1-78126-193-4
Mobi ISBN: 978-1-78126-194-1

The Publishers and author can accept no
responsibility for any consequences arising from
the information, advice or instructions given in
this publication.

Suppliers
If you have difficulty in obtaining any of the
materials and equipment mentioned in this book,
then please visit the Search Press website for
details of suppliers: www.searchpress.com

Printed in China

Dedication
To Trevor, Matthew, Jacob, Kate, Jeannine,
Niloufer and Claerwen for their patience,
encouragement and advice whilst I knitted
these projects.

Abbreviations

beg:	beginning
dec:	decrease
DPN:	double-pointed needles
g st:	garter stitch: knit every row
inc:	increase (by working into the front and back of the same stitch)
k:	knit
ktbl:	knit 1 row tbl
k2tog:	knit 2 stitches together
knitwise:	as though to knit
m:	make, usually make 1 additional stitch by knitting into the front and back of the same stitch
p:	purl
p2tog:	purl 2 stitches together
PM:	place marker
psso:	pass slipped stitch over
rem:	remaining
rep:	repeat
RS:	right side
sk2po:	slip 2 stitches knitwise on to right-hand needle, knit next stitch, then pass the previous slipped stitches over the knitted stitch
sl:	slip, usually slip 1 stitch
ssk:	slip 2 sts, then knit them together
st(s):	stitch(es)
st st:	stocking stitch (US stockinette stitch); alternate knit and purl rows (unless directed otherwise, always start with a knit row)
tbl:	through back loop
WS:	wrong side
wyrn:	wrap yarn around needle to create an extra stitch. (This makes up for the stitch you lose when you knit 2 together.)
yfrn:	yarn forward and over needle
yfwd:	yarn forward
yo:	yarn over
*:	repeat the instructions following the * as many times as specified

Contents

Introduction

This book is a collection of knitting patterns for wrist cuffs and wrist warmers. The patterns are easy to follow and are suitable for people who have mastered the basics in knitting. Practical, smart and great for all ages to wear, wrist warmers can be worn for warmth whether you are outdoors cycling, going on a country stroll, inside behind your office desk or just tucked up on the sofa at home.

I have had great fun knitting these wrist warmers in cafés, by the seaside and in the Highlands during my recent travels around both the UK and France, where I found inspiration to try new colours and textures.

The patterns in this book give the knitter the opportunity to try out new stitches such as cables, bobbles and simple lace, and to work in a range of yarns. The colours can be adapted to match your favourite garments, and the diversity of yarns means that this book contains wrist warmers suitable for all seasons.

Designing the cuffs gave me the opportunity to work with a variety of yarns with different textures, and I was able to extend my range of stitches to produce the variations of cuffs included in this book.

Wrist cuffs and warmers are not just for wrapping up during the winter – they can be a useful year-round accessory for those people who feel the cold.

There are wrist cuffs and wrist warmers in this book for men and women, and for both those with an unconventional style and the conventionally stylish. I hope you have many hours of pleasure knitting them.

Opposite:
This is a range of wrist warmers to suit all weathers and occasions. Choose your favourite colours and get knitting!

Knitting know-how

General notes

The wrist cuffs and wrist warmers in this book will fit an average-sized hand. The lengths are for guidance and can be adapted to suit individual tastes. If longer ones are preferred then you will require extra yarn.

Yarn

Most yarn today comes in hanks or skeins. These are big loops of yarn that are bought by weight and thickness. Before knitting they need to be wound into a ball so that the yarn does not get knotted. Some yarns can be bought ready-prepared as balls. These come in different weights and thicknesses and you can knit directly from them.

There are a variety of yarns used in the wrist cuff projects and these can be substituted for those of your choice. It is advisable to check the length and weight of yarn that you buy against the ones used in the patterns to ensure that you have enough to finish your projects.

Lace yarn (1–3 ply) is a very fine yarn that is used for more open patterns. Generally, you get very long meterage in a 50g ball or hank. In some of the patterns the lighter-weight yarns are doubled to create a more dense look and this has been noted on the individual pattern.

DK yarn (8-ply) is a medium thickness yarn that is suitable for many projects. The main DK yarn used in these projects is made from alpaca wool, with each ball containing 120m (131yd) of yarn.

Aran yarn (10-ply) is thicker than DK yarn and will produce cuffs that are thicker than those made with other weights.

Needles

Straight needles made from sustainable wood were used for all the projects in this book. I enjoy knitting with them because of their durability, and they are flexible to work with in all temperatures.

For many of the projects I used cable needles; these were also made from sustainable wood and I find that the yarns stay on them better than metal or plastic ones.

Other materials

For all of the projects you will need a pair of good-quality, sharp scissors to cut off the ends of yarns when sewing them into your work.

As well as knitting needles, you will also need a needle with a large eye (such as a tapestry needle) for sewing up all your projects.

Mattress stitch

Mattress stitch makes a practically invisible and nicely flexible seam for joining pieces together.

1 With the right sides of the cuffs facing, start with your yarn in the lower right corner. Take your needle across to the left edge and under the strand of yarn between the first and second stitches of the first row.

2 Take your needle back to the right edge and insert it one row up, between the first and second stitches of the row.

3 Take your needle back to the left edge and repeat stages one and two.

4 After completing a few stitches, gently pull the long end of the yarn to draw the stitches together.

This stitch will make your seam virtually invisible.

Cable cast on

This technique is used in patterns where you need to cast on in the middle of a row.

Insert your knitting needle between the first two stitches, wrap the yarn around your needle and bring it through to the front of your work. Transfer the newly created stitch onto the left-hand needle, thus increasing a stitch.

Tensions

All the tensions given for the yarns below are the manufacturer's guidelines for 10 x 10cm (4 x 4in) swatches knitted in stocking stitch (US stockinette stitch); these will be helpful if you decide to use alternative yarns to those used in the projects.

Yarns

Aran (10-ply)

Colinette Colourway: 67% wool, 33% cotton.

Tension: 14 sts x 19 rows using 6mm (UK 4/US 10) knitting needles.

Yardage: 100g hank/130m/142yd.

DK (8-ply)

UK Alpaca – Superfine Alpaca: 70% Alpaca, 30% Bluefaced Leicester.

Tension: 20 sts x 29 rows using 4mm (UK 8/US 6) knitting needles.

Yardage: 50g ball/120m/131yd.

UK Alpaca – Baby Alpaca and Silk Blend: 80% baby alpaca, 20% Tussah silk.

Tension: 20 sts x 29 rows using 4mm (UK 8/US 6) knitting needles.

Yardage: 50g ball/112m/122yd.

John Arbon Textiles – Knit by Numbers: 100% merino.

Tension: 22 sts x 28 rows using 4mm (UK 8/US 6) knitting needles.

Yardage: 100g hank/250m/273yd.

5 Moons Yarns – Diana DK: 50% superwash merino, 50% silk.

Tension: 20 sts x 28 rows using 4mm (UK 8/US 6) knitting needles.

Yardage: 100g hank/212m/232yd.

Rowan Baby Merino – Silk DK: 66% merino, 34% silk.

Tension: 22 sts x 30 rows using 4mm (UK 8/US 6) knitting needles.

Yardage: 50g ball/135m/148yd.

4-ply

Shilasdair Yarns – Luxury 4-ply: 10% cashmere, 10% baby camel, 40% angora, 40% merino lambswool.

Tension: 28 sts x 36 rows using 3.25mm (UK 10/US 3) needles.

Yardage: 50g hank/200m/219yd.

New Forest Mohair – Hand-dyed 4-ply: 100% mohair.

Tension: 18 sts x 28 rows using 4mm (UK 8/US 6) knitting needles.

Yardage: 100g hank/300m/328yd.

Blaze

Materials:

1 x 100g hank of aran (10-ply) yarn
 – variegated with a red base,
 130m/142yd

Needles:

1 pair of 5.5mm (UK 5/US 9)
 single-pointed knitting needles

Instructions:

Both cuffs are identical. Using 5.5mm (UK 5/US 9) needles, cast on 28 sts.

Rows 1–6: *k1, p1* repeat from * to * to end of row.

Rows 7–8: k1, *yo, k2tog*, rep from * to * to last st, k1.

Rows 9–10: Knit.

Rows 11–12: st st.

Rows 13–14: Knit.

Rows 15–16: st st.

Repeat rows 7–16 until work measures 18cm (7in), ending with a row 16.

Next row: k2tog *p1, k1*, rep from * to * to last 2 sts, p2tog.

Next two rows: *k1, p1*, rep from * to * to end of row.

Next row: Cast off all sts.

Making up

Using a tapestry needle and mattress stitch, join the seam 7cm (2¾in) from the finger end (cast-off) edge and 9cm (3½in) from the wrist end (cast-on) edge. This will leave a gap for your thumb to go through.

Weave in all loose ends.

These wrist warmers are simple to knit and the texture and colour of the yarn make them stand out from the crowd.

Bobble Tree

Materials:

2 x 50g balls of DK (8-ply) yarn in rose, each 120m/131yd

60cm (23½in) elastic

Needles:

1 pair of 3.5mm (UK 9 or 10/US 4) single-pointed knitting needles

1 pair of 4mm (UK 8/US 6) single-pointed knitting needles

Instructions:

Make two. Using 3.5mm (UK 9 or 10/US 4) needles, cast on 40 sts, then ktbl to form a neat edge.

Rib

Rows 1–2: *k1, p1*, rep from * to * to end of row. On row 2 of rib, inc 1 st in the middle of the row [41sts].

Change to 4mm (UK 8/US 6) needles.

Main pattern

Row 1 (RS): p2, *p6, k2tog, yfrn, p1, yo, sl1, k1, psso, p6*, p3, rep from * to * to last 2 sts, p2 [41sts].

Row 2: k2, *k6, p1, k3, p1, k6*, k3, rep from * to * to last 2 sts, k2.

Row 3: p2, *p5, k2tog, yfrn, p3, yo, sl1, k1, psso, p5*, p3, rep from * to * to last 2 sts, p2.

Row 4: k2, *(k5, p1) twice, k5*, k3, rep from * to * to last 2 sts, k2.

Row 5: p2, *p4, k2tog, yfrn, (p1, k1) twice, p1, yo, sl1, k1, psso, p4* p3, rep from * to * to last 2 sts, p2.

Row 6: k2, *k4, p1, k2, p1, k1, p1, k2, p1, k4*, k3, rep from * to * to last 2 sts, k2.

Row 7: p2, *p3, k2tog, yfrn, p2, k1, p1, k1, p2, yo, sl1, k1, psso, p3*, p3, rep from * to * to last 2 sts, p2.

Row 8: k2, *(k3, p1) twice, k1, (p1, k3) twice*, k3, rep from * to * to last 2 sts, k2.

Row 9: p2, *p2, k2tog, yfrn, p2, k2tog, yfrn, p1, yo, sl1, k1, psso, p2, yo, sl1, k1, psso, p2*, p3, rep from * to * to last 2 sts, p2.

Row 10: k2, *k2, (p1, k3) three times, p1, k2*, k3, rep from * to * to last 2 sts, k2.

Row 11 (bobble row): p2, *p2, (k1, p1, k1, p1) into next st, turn and p4, turn and k4, turn and p4, turn and sl1, k1, psso, k2tog, turn and p2tog, turn and slip bobble onto right-hand needle (bobble completed), p2, k2tog, yfrn, p3, yo, sl1, k1, psso, p2, make second bobble and slip it onto right-hand needle, p2*, p3, rep from * to * to last 2 sts, p2.

Row 12: k2, *(k5, p1) twice, k5*, k3, rep from * to * to last 2 sts, k2.

These are the 12 rows of your pattern.

Repeat these 12 rows twice more.

Change to 3.5mm (UK 9 or 10/US 4) needles.

Final rib

Row 1: *k1, p1*, rep from * to * to last 2 sts, p2tog.

Row 2: *k1, p1*, rep from * to * to end of row.

Cast off using the picot method as follows:

Cast off 2 sts, transfer 1 st on the right-hand needle to the left-hand needle, *cast on 2 sts using cable cast on, cast off 4 sts*, rep from * to * to the end of the row, casting off any odd sts remaining.

Making up

Join the seam using a tapestry needle and mattress stitch, 6.5cm (2½in) from the wrist end (cast-on edge) and 4cm (1½in) from finger end. This will leave a gap for your thumb to go through. Sew the elastic around the picot edge end for a snug fit around the fingers.

Weave in all loose ends.

These very pretty, lacy cuffs are made from the softest alpaca. They can be knitted in colours of your choice to complement your favourite clothes.

Breakfast at Tiffany's

Materials:

2 x 50g balls of DK (8-ply) yarn – 1 x lilac
(A), 1 x damson (B); both 120m/131yd

Needles:

1 pair of 4mm (UK 8/US 6) single-pointed
knitting needles

1 pair of 3.75mm (UK 9/US 5) single-pointed
knitting needles

Instructions:

Bobble

These instructions are for making a bobble,
abbreviated to (MB). All three sts are made
from the same st.

Row 1: knit into the front, back and front again
of the same st.

Row 2: p3, turn.

Row 3: sl1, k1, psso, k1, turn.

Row 4: p2tog, turn.

Right hand

Start at the border (finger end).

Using 3.75mm (UK 9/US 5) knitting needles
and yarn A, cast on 40 sts, then ktbl to form a
neat edge.

Rows 1–4: *k1, p1*, rep from * to * to end
of row.

Change to 4mm (UK 8/US 6) knitting needles
and start pattern as follows, decreasing 1 st on
first row only [40 sts].

Row 1: (k2, p2) three times, MB using colour B,
knit same st again using colour A, k1, p2, *k2,
p2*, rep from * to * to end of row.

Rows 2, 4 and 6: *p2, k2*, rep from * to * to end
of row.

Row 3: *k2, p2*, rep from * to * to end of row.

Row 5: As row 3.

Repeat the above six rows nine more times.
Cut off yarn A and change to 3.75mm (UK 9/
US 5) needles.

Next row: *k1, k2tog, k9, k2tog*, rep from * to *
twice, then k12.

Next two rows: *k1, p1*, rep from * to * to end
of row.

Cast off using small picot cast off as follows:

k2, cast off 1 st, *transfer st on right-hand
needle to left-hand needle and cast on 1 st
using cable cast on, cast off 2 sts*, rep from
* to * to end of row.

Left hand

As right hand until start of pattern (where you
change to 4mm (UK 8/US 6) needles), then
place bobbles as follows:

Row 1: *k2, p2*, rep from * to *seven times,
MB, (k2, p2) three times.

Continue with above spacing for bobbles using
the same row sequence as right glove.

Making up

Using a tapestry needle and mattress stitch,
join side seam 5.5cm (2¼in) from the finger
end and 8.5cm (3⅜in) from picot edge. This will
leave a gap for your thumb to go through.

Weave in all loose ends.

These handwarmers remind me of the film Breakfast at Tiffany's. They are elegant and warm, and can be knitted in colours of your choice.

Buttoned Cable Cuffs

Materials:

100g hank of DK (8-ply) merino yarn –
    variegated maroon, 250m/273yd

2 red buttons

Needles:

1 pair of 4.5mm (UK 7/US 7) single-pointed
    knitting needles

1 pair of 3.5mm (UK 9 or 10/US 4) single-
    pointed knitting needles

1 cable needle

Instructions:

Make two. Using 3.5mm (UK 9 or 10/US 4) knitting
needles, cast on 39 sts, then ktbl to form a neat edge.

Rows 1, 3, 5 and 7: *k2, p2*, rep from * to * to last 3 sts,
k2, p1.

Rows 2, 4 and 6: p1, k2, *p2, k2*, rep from * to * to end of row.

Row 8: *p4, inc1*, rep from * to * to last 3 sts, p3 [48 sts].

Main pattern

Change to 4.5mm (UK 7/US 7) knitting needles.

Rows 1 and 5: Knit.

Rows 2, 4 and 6: Purl.

Row 3: C6B (slip next 3 sts onto a cable needle and hold at back
of work, k next 3 sts from left-hand needle, then k sts from cable
needle), C6F (slip next 3 sts onto a cable needle and hold at
front of work, k the next 3 sts from left-hand needle, then k sts
from cable needle). Repeat the 12-stitch cable pattern three
more times.

Rep rows 1–6 seven times, until work measures 16cm (6¼in).

Next row: Knit.

Next row: *p6, p2tog*, rep from * to * to end of row [42 sts].

Next 6 rows: * k2, p2 * rep from * to * to last 2 sts, k2.

Cast off all sts.

Making up

With RS facing, join finger end (cast-on end) 6cm (2⅜in) from
the edge using a tapestry needle and mattress stitch. Join wrist
end, starting from the bottom of the border section 6.5cm (2½in)
down. This will leave a gap for your thumb to go through.

In this cuff there is an opening at the wrist end. Sew a button
at the centre of each glove on the border.

Weave in all loose ends.

These cuffs are knitted in a traditional cable stitch in a variegated yarn. I have added buttons to enhance the look.

Little Cable Cuffs

Materials:

2 x 50g balls of DK (8-ply) yarn – fawn,
120m/131yd

Needles:

1 pair of 4mm (UK 8/US 6) single-pointed
knitting needles

1 pair 4.5mm (UK 7/US 7) single-pointed
knitting needles

1 cable needle

Knitting note

Cr3F: slip next 2 sts onto a cable needle
and hold at front of work, p1, then k2 from
cable needle.

Cr3B: slip next st onto cable needle and
hold at back of work, k2, then p1 from
cable needle.

C4B: Place 2 sts on to a cable needle and
place at back of work. Knit next 2 sts, then
knit 2 sts from the cable needle.

C4F: Place 2 sts on to a cable needle and
place at front of work. Knit next 2 sts, then
knit 2 sts from the cable needle.

Instructions:

The pattern is the same for both hands, and
the yarn is used double throughout.

Using 4mm (UK 8/US 6) needles cast on 37 sts,
then ktbl to form a neat edge.

Row 1: *k1, p1*, rep from * to * to last st, k1.

Row 2: *p1, k1*, rep from * to * to last st, p1.

Rows 3–16: As rows 1 and 2, except inc 1 st at
the start and inc 1 st at the end of row 16 [39 sts].

Change to 4.5mm (UK 7/US 7) needles for the
following cable section of the pattern.

Rows 1, 3, 9 and 11: (WS) *p2, k2, p2, k1, p2, k2,
p2*, rep from * to * twice more.

Row 2: *k2, p2, slip next 3 sts onto cable needle
and hold at back of work, k2, slip the purl st
from cable needle back onto left-hand needle
and purl it, k2 from cable needle, p2, k2*, rep
from * to * twice more.

Rows 4 and 12: *Cr3F, Cr3B, p1, Cr3F, Cr3B*,
rep from * to * twice more.

Rows 5, 7, 13 and 15: *k1, p4, k3, p4, k1*, rep
from * to * twice more.

Rows 6 and 14: *p1, C4B, p3, C4F, p1*, rep from
* to * twice more.

Rows 8 and 16: *Cr3B, Cr3F, p1, Cr3B, Cr3F*,
rep from * to * twice more.

Row 10: *k2, p2, slip next 3 sts onto cable
needle and hold at front of work, k2, slip the
purl st from cable needle back onto left-hand
needle and purl it, k2 from cable needle, p2,
k2*, rep from * to * twice more.

Change to 4mm (UK 8/US 6) needles.

Row 17: *k2, p2*, rep from * to * to last 3 sts,
k2, p1.

Cast off all sts.

Making up

With RS facing, use a tapestry needle and
mattress stitch to join the side seams.

Weave in all loose ends.

These useful little cuffs will keep your hands warm on a winter's day, whether cycling, walking or working on a computer, as they allow you to have totally free hands. I have chosen a classic colour for this design and a gorgeous alpaca yarn, but they could equally well be knitted in a bright colour.

Caramel

Materials:

2 x 50g balls of DK (8-ply) alpaca/baby
merino yarn – 1 x butterscotch (A), 1 x ivory
(B); both 112m/122yd

Needles:

1 pair of 4mm (UK 8/US 6) single-pointed
knitting needles

1 pair 4.5mm (UK 7/US 7) single-pointed
knitting needles

Instructions:

Make two. Using 4mm (UK 8/US 6) needles
and yarn A, cast on 48 sts, then ktbl to form a
neat edge.

Rows 1 and 2: *k1, p1*, rep from * to * to end
of row.

Row 3: *k2A, k2B*, rep to end of row.

Row 4: p1B *p2A, p2B*, rep from * to * to last
3 sts, p2A, p1B.

Row 5: *k2B, k2A*, rep from * to * to end of row.

Rows 6 and 14: p1A, *p2B, p2A*, rep from *
to * to last 3 sts, p2B, p1A.

Rows 7, 13 and 17: As row 3.

Rows 8, 12 and 16: As row 4.

Rows 9, 11 and 15: As row 5.

Row 10: p1A, *p2B, p2A*, rep to last 3 sts,
p2B, p1A.

Repeat rows 1–10 of main pattern once more,
then rows 1–5 of main pattern once. The next
two rows follow the rib sequence you did in
rows 1 and 2 after the initial cast on.

Row 18: Purl, using yarn A.

Rows 19–20: st st, using yarn B.

Row 21: Knit, using yarn A, increasing 1 st at
both ends of the row [50sts].

Border

Change to 4.5mm (UK 7/US 7) needles.

Row 1: *p5A, p2B, p1A, p2B*, rep from * to *
to end of row.

Row 2: *k2B, k1A, k2B, k5A*, rep from * to *
to end of row.

Row 3: p2A, p1B, *p4A, p1B*, rep from * to * to
last 2 sts, p2A.

Row 4: As row 2.

Row 5: As row 1.

Row 6: *k5A, k2B, k1A, k2B*, rep from * to * to
end of row.

Row 7: *p2B, p1A, p2B, p5A*, rep from * to * to
end of row.

Row 8: k2A, *k1B, k4A*, rep from * to * to last
3 sts, k1B, k2A.

Row 9: *p2B, p1A, p2B, p5A*, rep from * to * to
end of row.

Row 10: As row 6.

Rep rows 1–10, then rep rows 1–5 once more.
Cut off yarn B and continue using yarn A only.

Change to 4mm (UK 8/US 6) needles.

Knit 1 row, decreasing 1 stitch at each end of
the row [48 sts].

Next 2 rows: k1, p1, rep from * to * to end of row.

Cast off all sts.

Making up

With RS facing and using a tapestry needle and
mattress stitch, join side seam 12cm (4¾in) from
the wrist end and 6cm (2⅜in) from the finger
end. This will leave a gap for your thumb to
go through.

Weave in all loose ends.

This pattern was inspired by a vintage pattern that I saw. I love the muted combination of colours, but this design would work equally well in bright colours.

Dainty Fair Isle

Materials:

3 x 50g balls of DK (8-ply) alpaca yarn –
   1 x midnight blue (A), 1 x mustard (B),
   1 x parchment (C); all 120m/131yd

Needles:

1 pair of 4mm (UK 8/US 6) single-pointed
   knitting needles

Instructions:

Make two. Using 4mm (UK 8/US 6) needles
and yarn A, cast on 40 sts, then ktbl to form a
neat edge.

Rows 1–2: *k1, p1*, rep from * to * to end of row.

Row 3: Using yarn B, knit, inc 4 sts evenly across the row
[44 sts].

Note that you are increasing only on row 3.

Row 4: Using yarn B, purl.

Rows 5 and 7: k1B, *k1A, k3B*, rep from * to * to last 3 sts,
k1A, k2B.

Row 6: *p1B, p1A*, rep from * to * to end of row.

Rows 8–9: Starting with a purl row and using yarn B, st st.

Rows 10 and 12: *p1A, p3B*, rep from * to * to end of row.

Row 11: *k1A, k1B*, rep from * to * to end of row.

Rows 13–14: Using yarn B, st st.

Rows 15–16: Using yarn A, knit. Cut off yarn A.

Rows 17–18: Using yarn C, knit.

Rows 19–30: Work as rows 3–14, substituting yarn C for yarn A.

Rows 31–32: Using yarn C, knit.

Rows 33–34: Using yarn A, knit.

Rows 35–46: As rows 3–14. Cut off yarn B.

Row 47: Using yarn A, knit.

Row 48: Cast off all sts.

Making up

Join side seams using a tapestry needle and mattress stitch, 7cm
(2¾in) from the wrist end (cast-on edge) and 5cm (2in) from the
finger end. This will leave a gap for your thumb to go through.

   Weave in all loose ends.

These cuffs are decorated with
a classic Fair Isle pattern. I have
chosen contemporary colours but
these could be adapted to suit
your taste.

Pretty Pastel

Materials:

3 x 50g balls of DK (8-ply) alpaca yarn –
   1 x parchment (A), 1 x rose pink (B),
   1 x sandstone (C); all 120m/131yd

Needles:

1 pair of 4mm (UK 8/US 6) single-pointed
   knitting needles

Knitting note

m1: pick up the loop between two sts to
make an additional st.

Instructions:

Right hand

Using 4mm needles and yarn A, cast on 40 sts,
then ktbl to form a neat edge.

Row 1: *k1, p1* rep from * to * to end of row
(RS).

Row 2: *p1, k1* rep from * to * to end of row.

Work eight more rows in rib, ending with a WS
row.

Shaping for thumb

Rows 11–12: st st yarn B.

Row 13: Using yarn B, k20, m1, k5, m1, k15 [42 sts].

Row 14: Using yarn B, purl.

Rows 15–16: Using yarn C, st st.

Row 17: k20, m1, k7, m1, k15 (at the same time
incorporating pattern), k1C, *k3A, k3C*, rep
from * to * until last stitch, k1A [44 sts].

Row 18: p1C, *p1A, p1C, p1A, p1C, p1B, p1C*,
rep from * to * to last st, k1A.

Row 19: As row 17, following the stitch
sequence without the increase.

Row 20: Using yarn C, purl.

Row 21: Using yarn C, k20, m1, k9, m1, k15
[46 sts]. Cut off yarn C.

Rows 22–24: Using yarn B, st st, starting with a
purl row.

Row 25: Using yarn B, k20, m1, k11, m1, k15
[48 sts].

Row 26: Using yarn A, purl.

Rows 27–28: Using yarn A, st st.

Divide for thumb

Next row (RS): Using yarn A, k33, turn.

Next row: Using yarn C, p13. Continue working
on these 13 sts only.

Row 1: Using yarn C, knit.

Row 2: p3C, p3A, p3C, p3A, p1C.

Row 3: *k1A, k1C, k1B, k1C, k1A, k1C*, rep
from * to * once more, then k1A.

Row 4: As row 2.

Rows 5–6: Using yarn C, st st. Cut off yarn C.

Row 7: Using yarn A, knit.

Row 8: Using yarn A, purl.

Sew side seam of thumb together.

Now rejoin yarn A. With RS facing, pick up two
stitches from the base of the thumb, then knit
to end of row [37 sts].

Next row: Using yarn C, purl.

Work st st over the next 13 rows in colours/
pattern as follows:

Row 1: Using yarn C, knit.

Row 2: *p3A, p3C*, rep from * to * to last st,
p1A.

Row 3: k1C, *k1A, k1C, k1A, k1C, k1B, k1C*,
rep from * to * to end of row

Row 4: As row 2.

Rows 5–6: Using yarn C, st st.

Rows 7–10: Using yarn A, st st. Cut off yarn A.

Rows 11–14: Using yarn B, st st.

Row 15: Using yarn C, *k1, p1*, rep from * to *
to last st, k1

Row 16: Using yarn C, *p1, k1*, rep from * to *
to last st, p1.

Cast off all sts.

Left hand

Work as for right hand up to the thumb shaping.

Rows 11–12: Using yarn B, st st.

Row 13: Using yarn B, k15, m1, k5, m1, k20 [42 sts].

Row 14: Using yarn B, purl.

Rows 15–16: st st, using yarn C.

Row 17: k15, m1, k7, m1, k20 (at the same time incorporating pattern), k1C, *k3A, k3C*, rep from * to * to last stitch, k1A [44 sts].

Row 18: p1C, *p1A, p1C, p1A, p1C, p1B, p1C*, rep from * to * to last st, p1A.

Row 19: As row 17, following the stitch sequence without the increase.

Row 20: Using yarn C, purl.

Row 21: Using yarn C, k15, m1, k9, m1, k20 [46 sts]. Cut off yarn C.

Rows 22–24: Using yarn B, st st, starting with a purl row.

Row 25: Using yarn B, k15, m1, k11, m1, k20 [48 sts].

Row 26: Using yarn A, purl.

Rows 27–28: Using yarn A, st st.

Divide for thumb

Next row (RS): Using yarn A, k33, turn.

Next row: Using yarn C, p13. Now continue working on these 13 sts only.

Work the thumb as for the right hand.

Continue working the pattern as for the right hand until the wrist cuff is complete.

Making up

With RS facing, sew up the side seam using a tapestry needle and mattress stitch.

Weave in all loose ends.

These wrist cuffs are made with a luxury alpaca in pastel colours and have a hint of Fair Isle in them.

Autumn

Materials:
4 x 50g balls of DK (8-ply) yarn – 1 x grey
(A), 1 x wine (B), 1 x mustard (C), 1 x
moss (D); all 120m/131yd

Needles:
1 pair of 4mm (UK 8/US 6) single-
pointed knitting needles

1 pair of 4.5mm (UK 7/US 7) single-
pointed knitting needles

Instructions:
Make two. Using 4mm (UK 8/US 6) needles and yarn A,
cast on 40 sts, then ktbl to form a neat edge.

Rows 1–2: *k1, p1*, rep from * to * to end of row.

Change to 4.5mm (UK 7/US 7) needles.

Row 3: *k2B, k2C*, rep from * to * to end of row.

Rows 4–7: Using yarn D, st st starting with a purl row. Cut off yarn D.

Row 8: *p2C, p2B*, rep from * to * to end of row.

Rows 9–12: Using yarn A, st st.

Rep rows 3–12 three more times and then rows 3–8 once more.

Border at the finger end
Change to size 4mm (UK 8/US 6) needles and, using yarn A, work
two rows in k1, p1 rib.

Cast off all sts.

Making up
With RS facing, join the side seam 8cm (3⅛in) from the wrist end
and 6cm (2⅜in) from the finger end, using a tapestry needle and
mattress stitch. This will leave a gap for your thumb to go through.

Weave in all loose ends.

These cuffs are very simple to make and I have used muted colours that blend in well together. Use the pattern to make a matching scarf to add style to your winter wardrobe.

Lilac

Materials:

1 x 100g hank of 4-ply (fingering) yarn –
purple variegated, 300m/328yd

1m (39in) narrow purple ribbon

Needles:

1 pair of 4mm (UK 8/US 6) single-
pointed knitting needles

1 pair of 3.25mm (UK 10/US 3) single-
pointed knitting needles

1 cable needle

Instructions:

Bell border

Make two. Using 3.25mm (UK 10/US 3) needles,
cast on 52 sts, then ktbl to form a neat edge.

Row 1 (RS): *p2, (k1, p1) four times, k1, p2*, rep
from * to * to end of row.

Row 2: *k2, (p1, k1) four times, p1, k2*, rep from
* to * to end of row.

Rows 3–4: Rep rows 1 and 2.

Row 5: *p2, k1, p1, ssk, k1, k2tog, p1, k1, p2*,
rep from * to * to end of row [44 sts].

Row 6: *k2, p1, k1, p3, k1, p1, k2*, rep from * to
* to end of row.

Row 7: *p2, k1, p1, sl2 knitwise, k1, pass the two
slipped sts over one at a time, p1, k1, p2*, rep
from * to * to end of row [36 sts].

Row 8: *k2, (p1, k1) twice, p1, k2*, rep from * to
* to end of row.

Row 9: *p2, ssk, k1, k2tog, p2*, rep from * to *
to end of row [28 sts].

Row 10: *k2, p3, k2*, rep from * to * to end
of row.

Row 11: *p2, sl next three sts onto a cable
needle, wrap yarn around the stitches twice,
then knit the stitches from the cable needle,
p2*, rep from * to * to end of row.

Row 12: *k2, p3, k2*, rep from * to * to end of
row.

Change to 4mm (UK 8/US 6) needles.

Next row: *k4, inc1, k1, inc1*, rep from * to * to
last 3 sts, knit to end of row [38 sts].

Next row: Purl.

Main pattern

Row 1: k2 *yfwd, k2tog* rep from * to * to last
2 sts, k2.

Row 2: Purl.

Continue working in st st until work measures
18.5cm (7¼in).

Change to 3.25mm (UK 10/US 3) needles.

Now rep rows 1 and 2 of main pattern.

Next row: k2tog, p1, *k1, p1*, rep from * to * to
last 3 sts, k2tog, p1 [36 sts].

Next row: *k1, p1*, rep from * to * to end of row.
Cast off all sts.

Making up

With RS facing, join the side seams using a
tapestry needle and mattress stitch, 7cm (2¾in)
from the wrist end, starting after the bell border
(the bell border will be left open) and 6cm
(2⅜in) from the finger end. This will leave a gap
for your thumb to go through.

Weave in all loose ends.

Thread the ribbon though every other gap
on the finger end, starting the threading at
the centre front. Tie the ribbon together with
a bow.

These feminine wrist warmers are made in a fine mohair with a pretty border and ribbon edging.

Mondrian

Materials:

3 x 100g hanks of DK (8-ply) merino yarn –
  1 x red (A), 1 x yellow (C), 1 x green (E); all
  250m/273yd

2 x 50g balls of DK (8-ply) alpaca yarn – 1 x
  black (B), 1 x white (D); both 120m/131yd

Needles:

1 pair of 4mm (UK 8/US 6) single-pointed
  knitting needles

Knitting note

m1: pick up the loop between two sts and
work into the back of it.

Instructions:

The yarn is used double throughout. Twist the
yarn every 3 sts to avoid large loops across the
back of your work.

Right hand

Using 4mm (UK 8/US 6) needles and yarn A,
cast on 40 sts, then ktbl to form a neat edge.

Rows 1–14: *k2, p2*, rep from * to * to end of row.

Shaping for thumb

Row 15: Using yarn B, k20, m1, k5, m1, k15
[42 sts].

Row 16: Purl.

The Mondrian-style colour blocks are done over
6 rows, so whether you are knitting or purling,
the colour changes take place at the same point.

Row 17: k8C, k4B, k6D, k8B, k6C, k10B.

Row 18: Purl, following the same colour
sequence as row 17.

Row 19: k8C, k4B, k6D, k2B, m1, k6B, k1C, m1,
k5C, k10B [44 sts].

Rows 20–22: st st, starting with a purl row, and
following the same colour sequence as row 19.

Row 23: Using yarn A, k20, m1, k9, m1, k15 [46 sts].

Row 24: Purl.

Row 25: k8D, k4B, k16D, k3B, k8D, k4B, k3D.

Row 26: Purl, following the same colour
sequence as row 25.

Row 27: k8D, k4B, k8D, m1, k8D, k3B, m1, k8D,
k4B, k3D [48 sts].

Rows 28–30: st st, starting with a purl row, and
following the same colour sequence as row 27.

Divide for thumb

Row 31: Using yarn B, (RS) k33, turn. Cut off
yarn D.

Row 32: p13 using yarn B.

Rows 33–38: Working on these 13 sts only, work
6 rows in st st, using yarn B.

Row 39: *k2, p2*, rep from * to * to last st, k1.

Row 40: p1, *k2, p2* rep from * to * to end
of row.

Cast off all sts.

Using a tapestry needle and mattress stitch,
sew side seams of thumb together.

With RS facing and yarn B, rejoin yarn and pick
up and knit 2 sts from base of thumb then knit
to end of row [37 sts].

Row 42: Purl, using yarn B.

Row 43: k15E, k5B, k6D, k4B, k7C.

Rows 44–48: Starting with a purl row, st st,
following the same colour sequence as row 43.

Rows 49–50: st st, using yarn A.

Row 51: k4B, k6D, k8C, k5B, k8D, k6C.

Rows 52–56: Starting with a purl row, st st,
following the same colour sequence as row 51.
Cut off all yarns except yarn A.

Row 57: Knit, using yarn A.

Row 58: *k2, p2*, rep from * to * to last st, k1.

Row 59: p1, *k2, p2*, rep from * to * to end
of row.

Cast off all sts following rib pattern of last 2
rows. Cut off yarn, leaving a sufficient length to
sew up the side seam.

Left hand

Work as for right hand to the thumb shaping.

Row 15: Using yarn B, k15, m1, k5, m1, k20 [42 sts].

Row 16: Purl.

Row 17: k10B, k6C, k8B, k6D, k4B, k8C [42 sts].

Row 18: Purl, following the same colour
sequence as row 17.

Row 19: k10B, k5C, m1, k1C, k6B, m1, k2B, k6D,
k4B, k8C [44 sts].

Rows 20–22: st st, starting with a purl row, and
following the same colour sequence as row 19.

Row 23: Using yarn A, k15, m1, k9, m1, k20 [46 sts].

Row 24: Purl.

Row 25: k3D, k4B, k8D, k3B, k16C, k4B, k8D, [46 sts].

Row 26: Purl, following the same colour sequence as row 25.

Row 27: k3D, k4B, k8D, m1, k3B, k8D, m1, k8C, k4B, k8D [48 sts].

Rows 28–30: st st, starting with a purl row and following the same colour sequence as row 27.

Divide for thumb

Row 31: (RS) Using yarn B, k28, turn.

Row 32: p13.

Rows 33–40: work as for right hand from rows 33–40.

Cast off all sts. With RS facing, rejoin yarn and pick up and knit 2 sts from base of thumb, then knit to end of row [37 sts].

Row 42: Using yarn B, purl.

Row 43: k7C, k4B, k6D, k5B, k15E.

Rows 44–48: st st, starting with a purl row and following the same colour sequence as row 43.

Rows 49–50: Using yarn A, st st.

Row 51: k6C, k8D, k5B, k8C, k6D, k4B.

Rows 52–56: st st, starting with a purl row and following the same colour sequence as row 51. Cut off all yarns except yarn A.

Row 57: Using yarn A, knit.

Row 58: *k2, p2*, rep from * to * to last st, k1.

Row 59: p1, *k2, p2*, rep from * to * to end of row.

Cast off all sts following rib pattern of last 2 rows. Cut off yarn, leaving a sufficient length to sew up the side seam.

Making up

Sew up side seams, with RS facing, using a tapestry needle and mattress stitch. Match the colours as you sew. Weave in all loose ends.

The geometric design of these gloves makes them rather eye-catching. They were inspired by an exhibition I saw featuring the Dutch artist, Mondrian, and are knitted using a Fair Isle technique combined with intarsia.

Parisienne

Materials:

2 x 50g balls of DK (8-ply) yarn – 1 x lilac
  (A), 1 x damson (B); both 120m/131yd

Needles:

1 pair of 4mm (UK 8/US 6) single-pointed
  knitting needles

Instructions:

Make two.

Frill

Row 1: Using 4mm (UK8/US 6) needles and
yarn A, cast on 2 sts.

Row 2: k1, m1, k1 [3 sts].

Row 3: p3.

Row 4: k1, m1, k1, m1, k1 [5 sts].

Row 5: k1, yo, k2tog, yo, k2tog.

Next rows: Repeat rows 1–5 seven more times
[40 sts].

Main body of wrist warmer

Rows 1–2: Using yarn A, *k1, p1*, rep from * to *
to end of row. Cut off yarn A.

Row 3: Using yarn B, knit, increasing 1 st in the
middle of the row [41 sts].

Rows 4–6: Using yarn B and starting with a purl
row, st st.

Rows 7–10: k1, *p1, k1*, rep from * to * to end
of row.

Row 11: k1, *yfwd, sl1, k1, psso, k3, k2tog, yfwd,
k1*, rep from * to * to end of row.

Row 12: Purl.

Row 13: k2, *yfwd, sl1, k1, psso, k1, k2tog, yfwd,
k3*, rep from * to * to last 7 sts, yfwd, sl1, k1,
psso, k1, k2tog, yfwd, k2.

Row 14: Purl.

Row 15: k3, *yfwd, sl1, k2tog, psso, yfwd, k5*,
rep from * to * to last 6 sts, yfwd, sl1, k2tog,
psso, yfwd, k3.

Row 16: Purl.

Rep rows 7–16 four more times and then rows
7–10 once more.

Cast off all sts.

Making up

When making up these wrist warmers, you will
join the cast-off edge to the edge where the frill
is. Note that the frill overlaps the seam.

Using a tapestry needle and mattress stitch,
join the side seam 5cm (2in) from the top,
matching the cast-off edge to the start of the
frill (where the colours change).

Join the bottom of the cuff 9.5cm (3¾in) from
the wrist end. This will leave a gap for your
thumb to go through. Weave in all loose ends.

This chic little pair of wrist warmers was inspired by a recent visit to Paris. They have a fun element as well as keeping your hands warm.

Tiger Ruche

Materials:
2 x 50g hanks of 4-ply yarn – 1 x gold (A),
  1 x warm red (B); both 200m/219yd

Needles:
1 pair of 3.25mm (UK 10/US 3) single-pointed
  knitting needles

Instructions:
Make two.

Cuff frill
Using 3.25mm (UK 10/US 3) needles and yarn
A, cast on 84 sts, then ktbl to form a neat edge.

Row 1: Knit.

Row 2: Purl.

Row 3: Knit.

Row 4: *p2tog*, rep from * to * to end of row
[42 sts].

Main cuff pattern
Row 1: Using yarn B, (k1, sl1) four times, k10,
sl1, (k1, sl1) three times, k10, (k1, sl1) three
times, k1.

> #### Knitting note
> After the first row of the pattern you might
> find it helpful to knit through the back of the
> sts of the striped sections on the knit rows,
> and slip the slip sts from the back on the purl
> row. It will work if you do it the conventional
> way, but it will be a little more difficult.

Row 2: Using yarn B, (p1, sl1) three times, p10,
(p1, sl1) four times, p10, (sl1, p1) four times.

Row 3: Using yarn A, sl1, (k1, sl1) three times,
k11, (k1, sl1) three times, k11, (sl1, k1) three
times, sl1.

Row 4: Using yarn A, (sl1, p1) three times,
sl1, p11, (sl1, p1) three times, p10, (p1, sl1)
four times.

Repeat rows 1–4 of pattern until work measures
19cm (7½in), (20 x 4 row pattern repeats). Cut
off yarn A.

Cast off with yarn B, using the picot method as
follows:

Cast off 2 sts, transfer 1 st on right-hand needle
to left-hand needle, *cast on 2 sts using cable
cast-on, cast off 4 sts*, rep from * to * to end of
row, casting off any odd stitches remaining.

Making up
Join the frill at the wrist end, so that it overlaps
the pattern by approximately 1.5cm (½in).
Using mattress stitch, with RS facing, join the
side seam 8.5cm (3⅜in) from the base of the
cuff. Join the seam at the finger end, 5cm (2in)
from the picot edge. This will leave a gap for
your thumb. Weave in all loose ends.

These are funky little cuffs that are ruched to make them very feminine. I have chosen autumnal colours as I think they would look great with big woolly jumpers. The picot edging adds a certain panache.

Scallop

Materials:
1 x 100g hank of DK (8-ply) merino yarn –
   burnt orange; 250m/273yd

Needles:
1 pair of 3.75mm (UK 9/US 5) single-pointed
   knitting needles

1 pair of 4.5mm (UK 7/US 7) single-pointed
   knitting needles

1 cable needle

Instructions:
Make two.

Using 3.75mm (UK 9/US 5) needles, cast on
39 sts.

Border
Row 1: (RS) *k1, yo, k4, sk2po, k4, yo, k1*, rep
from * to * to end of row.

Row 2: *p2 ,k9, p2*, rep from * to * to end of
row.

Row 3: *k2, yo, k3, sk2po, k3, yo, k2*, rep from
* to * to end of row.

Row 4: *p3, k7, p3*, rep from * to * to end of
row.

Row 5: *k3, yo, k2, sk2po, k2, yo, k3*, rep from
* to * to end of row.

Row 6: *p4, k5, p4*, rep from * to * to end of
row.

Row 7: *k4, yo, k1, sk2po, k1, yo, k4*, rep from
* to * to end of row.

Row 8: *p5, k3, p5*, rep from * to * to end of
row.

Row 9: *k5, yo, sk2po, yo, k5*, rep from * to *
to end of row.

Row 10: Purl.

Change to 4.5mm (UK 7/US 7) needles.

Weave pattern
Row 1: Knit (first time only inc 7 sts evenly
across row) [46 sts].

Rows 2, 4 and 6: Purl.

Row 3: *Work right crossover on 4 sts as
follows: slip 2 sts onto cable needle and hold at
back of work, k2, then k2 from cable needle*,
rep from * to * to last 2 sts, k2.

Row 5: k2, *work left crossover on 4 sts as
follows: slip 2 sts onto cable needle and hold at
front of work, k2, then k2 from cable needle*,
rep from * to * to end of row.

Repeat rows 1–6 until work measures 19cm
(7½in).

Change to 3.75mm (UK 9/US 5) needles.

Next row: k4, *k2tog, k7*, rep from * to * to the
last 6 sts, k2tog, k4.

Cast off all sts.

Making up
With RS facing, use a tapestry needle and
mattress stitch to join the side seams 5cm (2in)
up from the finger end opening. Leave a gap of
6cm (2⅜in) and then join the seam to the base
of the border. This will leave the border open at
the wrist end.

Weave in all loose ends.

These cuffs are knitted using a simple cable and I have added a pretty border to give them a unique touch. I love the burnt orange colour, but you can choose your own favourite colour to make them.

Heathland

Materials:
1 x 100g hank of DK (8-ply) merino yarn –
variegated; 212m/232yd

Needles:
1 pair of 3.5mm (UK 9 or 10/US 4) single-
pointed knitting needles

1 pair of 4mm (UK 8/US 6) single-pointed
knitting needles

Instructions:
Make two.

Using size 3.5mm (UK 9 or 10/US 4) needles, cast
on 40 sts, then ktbl to form a neat edge.

Rows 1 and 2: Knit.

Change to 4mm (UK 8/US 6) needles.

Main pattern
Row 1: Knit, inc 3 sts evenly across the row [43 sts].

Row 2 and all even-numbered rows: Work each st as it appears
from this side of the work (i.e. knit the k sts and purl the p sts).
Purl the loops made in the row below.

Rows: 3, 11 and 13: Knit.

Rows 5, 7 and 9: p1, *yfrn, k4, sl1, k1, psso, p1, k2tog, k4, yfrn,
p1*, rep from * to * to end of row.

Rows 15, 17 and 19: p1, *k2tog, k4, yfrn, p1, yfrn, k4, sl1, k1, psso,
p1*, rep from * to * to end of row.

Rep rows 1–20 twice.

Next rows: Change to 3.5mm (UK 9 or 10/US 4) needles and rep
rows 1 and 2. On row 2, dec 3 sts evenly across the row [40 sts].

Cast off using the picot cast off as follows: cast off 2 sts, *slip
stitch on right-hand needle on to left-hand needle, cast on 2
stitches using cable method, cast off 4 sts*. Rep from * to * to
end of row. Fasten off last stitch.

Making up
Join side seams 5cm (2in) from the top (picot edge) and 7cm
(2¾in) from the bottom. This will leave a gap for your thumb to
go through.

Weave in all loose ends.

These pretty cuffs were inspired by the beautiful colours of a silky variegated yarn I found. The tones remind me of a visit to Scotland, where I saw the lovely hues of the heathers and ferns.

Frosty

Materials:

3 x 100g hank of DK (8-ply) merino yarn – 1 x red (A), 1 x white (B), 1 x black (C); all 250m/273yd

Needles:

1 pair of 4mm (UK 8/US 6) single-pointed knitting needles

Instructions:

Make two. The black yarn is used double throughout to accentuate the snowman's hat and buttons.

Using 4mm (UK 8/US 6) needles and yarn A, cast on 40 sts, then ktbl to form a neat edge.

Rows 1–16: *k1, p1*, rep from * to * to end of row.

Rows 17–18: st st.

Row 19: k2A, *k1B, k4A*, rep from * to * to last pattern rep, k2A.

Row 20: p1A, *p3B, p2A*, rep from * to * to last pattern rep, p1A.

Row 21: *k2B, k1A, k2B*, rep from * to * to end of row.

Row 22: As row 20.

Row 23: As row 19. Cut off yarn B.

Rows 24–26: st st in yarn A.

Row 27: Work row 1 of the chart, placing the 2 snowmen motifs as follows: k7A, k7B, k12A, k7B, k7A to set the spacing, then continue to work rows 2–26 from chart. Cut off yarns B and C.

Next 2 rows: st st, using yarn A.

Next 2 rows: *k1, p1*, rep to end of row.

Cast off all sts.

Making up

With RS facing, use a tapestry needle and mattress stitch to join the side seams, 10cm (4in) from the wrist end and 5cm (2in) from the finger end. This will leave a gap for your thumb to go through.

Weave in all loose ends.

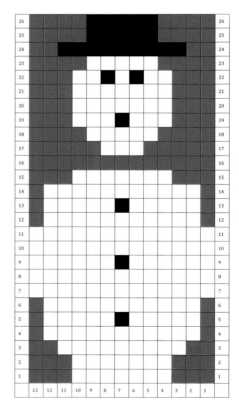

Everyone loves snowmen. I have knitted the motif using intarsia to avoid large loops at the back of the work, and cut-off lengths of white and black yarn to make the knitting easier.

Sparkler

Materials:

1 x 100g skein of DK (8-ply) beaded yarn –
turquoise; 250m/273yd

Needles:

1 pair of 4mm (UK 8/US 6) single-pointed
knitting needles

1 pair of 3.5mm (UK 9 or 10/US 4) single-
pointed knitting needles

Instructions:

Make two. Using 4mm (UK 8/US 6) needles, cast
on 37 sts, then ktbl to form a neat edge.

Next row: k3 *MB, k5*, rep from * to * to last 4
sts, MB, k3.

MB: Make a bobble all in the same stitch. Knit
into front, back and front again of same st, turn.
Sl1, k1, psso, k1, pass previous st over. You are
now back to the original 1 stitch.

Main pattern

Row 1 and every odd-numbered row (WS): Purl.

Row 2: *k10, sl1, k1, psso, yfwd*, rep from * to *
to last st, k1.

Row 4: k9, sl1, k1, psso, yfwd, *k10, sl1, k1, psso,
yfwd*, rep from * to * to last 2 sts, k2.

Row 6: *k8, (sl1, k1, psso, yfwd) twice*, rep from
* to * to last st, k1.

Row 8: k7, (sl1, k1, psso, yfwd) twice, *k8, (sl1,
k1, psso, yfwd) twice*, rep from * to * to last 2
sts, k2.

Row 10: *k6, (sl1, k1, psso, yfwd) three times*,
rep from * to * to last st, k1.

Row 12: k5, (sl1, k1, psso, yfwd) three times, *k6,
(sl1, k1, psso, yfwd) three times*, rep from * to *
to last 2 sts, k2.

Row 14: *k4, (sl1, k1, psso, yfwd) four times*, rep
from * to * to last st, k1.

Row 16: k1, *yfwd, k2tog, k10*, rep from * to *
to end of row.

Row 18: k2, yfwd, k2tog, *k10, yfwd, k2tog*, rep
from * to * to last 9 sts, k9.

Row 20: k1, *(yfwd, k2tog) twice, k8*, rep from *
to * to end of row.

Row 22: k2, (yfwd, k2tog) twice, *k8, (yfwd,
k2tog) twice*, rep from * to * to last 7 sts, k7.

Row 24: k1, *(yfwd, k2tog) three times, k6*, rep
from * to * to end of row.

Row 26: k2, (yfwd, k2tog) three times, *k6 (yfwd,
k2tog) three times*, rep from * to * to last 5
sts, k5.

Row 28: k1, *(yfwd, k2tog) four times, k4*, rep
from * to * to end of row.

Repeat rows 1–17 once more.

Change to 3.5mm (UK 9 or 10/US 4) needles.

Next row: *k1, p1*, rep from * to * to last st, k1.

Next row: p1, *k1, p1*, rep from * to * to end
of row.

Cast off all stitches.

Making up

Join the side seams using a tapestry needle
and mattress stitch, 7cm (2¾in) from the wrist
end (cast-on edge) and 5cm (2in) from the
finger end. This will leave a gap for your
thumb to go through.

Weave in all loose ends.

These are really pretty beaded cuffs that will brighten up any outfit. The bobbles around the cuff add a little more texture to the fabric.

Chic Stripes

Materials:

2 x 100g hanks of DK (8-ply) merino yarn – 1 x light grey (A), 1 x dark grey (B); both 250m/273yd

2 small, striped buttons

Needles:

1 pair of 4mm (UK 8/US 6) single-pointed knitting needles

Instructions:

Right hand

Using 4mm (UK 8/US 6) needles and yarn A, cast on 40 sts, then ktbl to form a neat edge.

Rows 1–2: *k2, p2*, rep from * to * to end of row.

Change to yarn B. From this point on, change colours every two rows to form the stripes.

Rows 3–14: st st.

Shape for thumb

Row 15: k20, m1, k5, m1, k15 [42 sts].

Rows 16–18: st st, starting with a purl row.

Row 19: k20, m1, k7, m1, k15 [44 sts].

Rows 20–22: st st, starting with a purl row.

Row 23: k20, m1, k9, m1, k15 [46 sts].

Rows 24–26: st st, starting with a purl row.

Row 27: k20, m1, k11, m1, k15 [48 sts].

Rows 28–30: st st, starting with a purl row.

Divide for thumb

Row 31: (RS) k33, turn.

Row 32: p13.

Rows 33–38: Working on these 13 sts only, knit in st st, continuing in the stripe sequence.

Row 39: *k2, p2*, rep from * to * to last st, k1.

Row 40: p1, *k2, p2*, rep from * to * to end of row.

Cast off all sts.

Using a tapestry needle and mattress stitch, sew the side seam of the thumb. With RS facing, rejoin yarn and pick up and knit 2 sts from the base of the thumb, then knit to end of row [37 sts].

Next row: Purl.

Next 15 rows: st st.

Knitting note

m1: knit the loop between two sts.

Next row: *k2, p2*, rep from * to * to last st, k1.

Next row: p1, *k2, p2*, rep from * to * to end of row. Cut off yarn B.

Cast off all sts following rib pattern.

Left hand

Work as for right hand up to the shaping of the thumb.

Row 15: k15, m1, k5, m1, k20 [42 sts].

Rows 16–30: Work increases as for right hand using the spacing of row 15 above – start increase rows with k15 sts and end with k20 sts.

Divide for thumb

Next row: (RS) k28, turn.

Next row: p13.

Next 8 rows: As for right-hand thumb.

Cast off and join the side seam of the thumb. With RS facing, rejoin yarn and pick up and knit 2 sts from base of thumb, then knit to end of row.

Next row: Purl.

Next 15 rows: st st.

Next row: *k2, p2*, rep from * to * to last st, k1.

Next row: p1, *k2, p2*, rep from * to * to end of row. Cut off yarn B.

Cast off all sts following rib pattern.

Bow (make four)

Cast on 13 sts using 4mm (UK 8/US 6) needles and yarn A, then ktbl to form a neat edge.

Rows 1–2: st st.

Cast off all sts. Weave in all loose ends.

Making up

With RS facing, use a tapestry needle and mattress stitch to sew up the side seams. Match the stripes as you sew up your gloves. Weave in all loose ends.

Place bows on the front of the glove, three light grey stripes down from the finger end. Cross the strips in the centre and place a small, striped button in the middle. Sew the button in place using yarn B (this will also secure the bow onto the glove).

These pretty little gloves will keep your hands warm on a winter's day. I have chosen muted greys for the stripes, but they would be equally pretty in bright or subtle colours.

Sunshine

Materials:

1 x 100g hank of DK (8-ply) merino yarn –
golden yellow; 250m/273yd

Needles:

1 pair of 4mm (UK 8/US 6) single-pointed
knitting needles

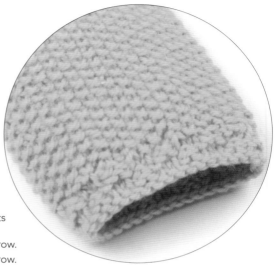

Instructions:

Make two.

Using 4mm (UK 8/US 6) needles, cast on 40 sts
then ktbl to form a neat edge.

Rows 1–2: *k2, p2*, rep from * to * to end of row.

Rows 3–4: *p2, k2*, rep from * to * to end of row.

Rows 5–6: As rows 1 and 2.

Rows 7–8: As rows 3 and 4.

Row 9: *k1, p1*, rep from * to * to end of row.

Row 10: *p1, k1*, rep from * to * to end of row.

Next rows: Rep rows 9 and 10 until work measures 19cm (7½in).

Finger end

Row 1: k2, p2, k2tog, k1, *p2, k2, p2, k1, k2tog*, rep from * to *
to last 6 sts, p2, k2, p2.

Row 2: *k2, p2*, rep from * to * to end of row.

Rows 3–4: *p2, k2*, rep from * to * to end of row.

Cast off all sts.

Making up

Join the seam 5cm (2in) from the finger end, using a tapestry
needle and mattress stitch, then 10cm (4in) from the wrist end.
The gap between the seams is the space for your thumb.

Weave in all loose ends.

This pair of simple wrist warmers can be made by anyone who has mastered knitting basics. They can be knitted in any colour of DK yarn to match your favourite garments.

Playful

Materials:

2 x 50g balls of DK (8-ply) super fine alpaca yarn – parchment; 250m/273yd

2 black buttons

Needles:

1 pair of 4.5mm (UK 7/US 7) single-pointed knitting needles

1 pair of 5mm (UK 6/US 8) single-pointed knitting needles

1 cable needle

Instructions:

Make two. The yarn is used double throughout.

Using 4.5mm (UK 7/US 7) needles, cast on 34 sts, then ktbl to form a
neat edge.

Rows 1–2: *k1, p1*, rep from * to * to end of row.

Change to 5mm (UK 6/US 8) needles and start 12-row pattern; inc 1 st at beginning and 1 st at end of the first row only [36 sts].

Rows 1 and 11: *k3, p1, k1, p1, k1, p1, k1*, rep from * to * to end of row.

Rows 2, 10 and 12: *k1, p1, k1, p1, k1, p1, p3*, rep from * to * to end of row.

Row 3: *k3, slip 3 sts onto a cable needle and place at front of work, k1, p1, k1, then p1, k1, p1 from cable needle*, rep from * to * to end of row.

Rows 4, 6 and 8: *p1, k1, p1, k1, p1, k1, p3*, rep from * to * to end of row.

Rows 5 and 7: *k3, k1, p1, k1, p1, k1, p1*, rep from * to * to end of row.

Row 9: k3, slip next 3 sts onto a cable needle and place at front of work, p1, k1, p1, then k1, p1, k1 from cable needle*, rep from * to * to end of row.

Rep rows 1–12, then rep rows 1–10 once more.

Change to 4.5mm (UK 7/US 7) needles.

Decrease by k2tog evenly across the next row. The decreases take place on the first row of the final rib only.

Next row (wrist end): *k1, p1* rep from * to * to end of row.

Rep above row once more, then cast off all sts.

Making up

With RS facing, use a tapestry needle and mattress stitch to join the side seams, 5cm (2in) from the finger end and 6cm (2⅜in) from the wrist end. Using spare yarn, add a button to embellish each wrist cuff.

Weave in all loose ends.

These little cuffs combine a panel of stocking stitch with a crossover textured moss stitch. Knit them in a colour of your choice and customise them by adding a button.

Acknowledgements
My thanks to Colinette Colourway,
Jillybean Yarns, Erika Knight, Debonnaire, New
Forest Mohair and Juliet at John Arbon. My special
thanks to Chas and Rachel at UK Alpaca, who have
supported me for the majority of my projects.
I would also like to thank Search Press for
asking me to write my third book for them.
*For yarns and other patterns, visit the author's
website: www.theknitknacks.co.uk*

Publishers' Note
If you would like more information on knitting techniques try:
Knitting for the Absolute Beginner by Alison Dupernex,
Search Press, 2012;
Twenty to Make: Easy Knitted Scarves by Monica Russel,
Search Press, 2013